The Celebrity WHO'S WHO OF LOSERS

INTERNATIONAL LOSERS CLUB®

— A PARODY —

The Celebrity WHO's WHO OF LOSERS

A PARODY

 **GORDON** ENTERTAINMENT MULTIMEDIA, INC.
New York, NY

Published by

Gordon Entertainment Multimedia, Inc.
EMPIRE STATE BUILDING
350 Fifth Avenue - Suite 3304
New York, NY 10118-0069

Cover and interior illustrations by Comic Relief, Inc.

ISBN: 0-9647318-2-7

Printed in the United States of America

THE RESULTS ARE IN!

The membership of
The International Losers Club
has spoken!!

We polled our members - all accomplished and experienced losers in their own right - to find out who *they* considered to be the world's biggest losers in entertainment, politics and news events.

The International Losers Club is now proud to present the first edition of *The Celebrity Who's Who of Losers.*TM

Editorial Board of Losers

Acknowledgments

Thanks to the following people for all their support.

Odie J., Ed E., Brian S.S, Mike F., Jaime O., L.P.R., Jackie L., Ted C., Kurt J., Walter S., Brian, Stacy, Andrew, Benjamin, Heather, Jennifer, Harrison, Traci, Cherilyn, Laci & Coco B. Gordon, Tom F., Debbie M., Kim M., Marie F., Amy S., Scott D., Curtis S., Doug R., Jim K., Judie G., Paul & Sylvia, Gino R., Bill C., Fran M., Mitch M., Joanne & Mary, Mike D., Gary P., Donnalisa A., Nick & Athena G., Linda C., Apryl G., Rona L., David H., Marie & Missy, Joel S., Tony C., Ray R., Alan C., Juliette M., Veronica P., Al R., Wayne M., Marcia T., Lynette D., Mike T., Fran A., Cindy L., Marlys R., Chris & Marshall C., Diane & John P., Karen L., Sharon L.R., Sue S., Kate B., Kathy O.,Larry C., Susan C., Lisa C.G., Lou & Angie B., Don & Hope B., Mike & Andie M., Tom & JoAnn P., David & Ruth K., Jill R., Josh H., Lou V., Helen C., Sharon G., Leo & Lisa K., Monica O., Bob G., Myrtle & Don G., Del A., Tony B., Brian M., Steven & David J., Burton G., Jim T., Mona M., Steven B., Robert S., Stephen S., Claudia C., Suzan A., Doug W., Debbie S., Lori M., Bea K., Rhonda P., Claudia K., Caren K., Karen L., Chris M.

Contents

Headline Losers

Joey Buttafuoco

a.k.a. - "Jailbait Joey"

While it's true that lots of guys score with their teenage girlfriends on Prom night, those guys usually aren't married and middle aged.

Joey used to run an auto body shop where he reportedly spent most of his time in the back seats of cars putting mileage on his high school honey.

As if Hollywood didn't already have enough no-talent egomaniacs, Joey has packed up and moved to California to pursue an acting career. He was asked to demonstrate his acting ability by reading the following lines:

- "Judge, I swear I didn't know she was 16."

- "Officer, I wasn't trying to buy sex from a hooker, I was just asking for directions. I asked if she knew how we could get to a hotel room."

- "Mary Jo, I love you."

Hey Joey, we have some friendly advice for you:

From now on, you *Buttafuoco* someone your own age!

Least favorite song: Go Away Little Girl

Likes: The "show and tell" method of explaining the facts of life

Dislikes: Helping his dates with their math homework

2

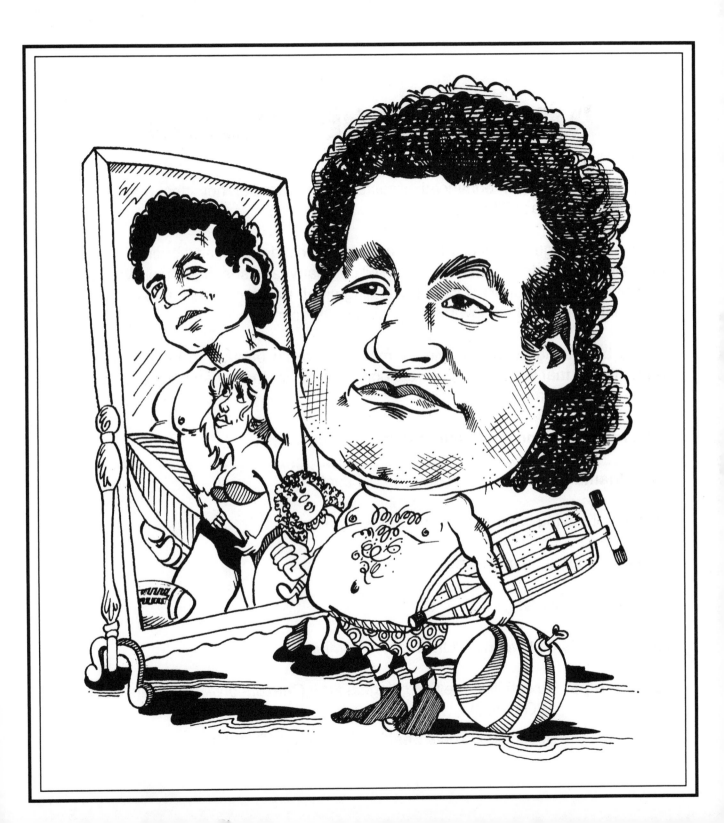

Anna Nicole Smith

With her surgically enhanced breasts, it's no wonder her cleavage is more commonly known as "Silicone Valley."

This gold digger struck oil when she married the elderly Texas tycoon, J. Howard Marshall II. The octogenarian owned an oil company (and she thought oil was called a "fossil" fuel in his honor). On their wedding night, everyone was left to ponder the mathematical question, "How many times can 89 go into 26?"

The best thing about marrying a man who is old enough to be your father's grandfather is that you can buy him a single condom for the honeymoon and be sure that he has a lifetime supply.

Her former husband's petname for her: Cuddles

Her petname for him: Die already you old coot!

Hobbies: Leaving banana peels near open graves

Dislikes: Heart lung machines

Likes: Power failures

Her husband's last words: "Oh God, I'm coming."

Memberships: Buxom Illiterate Gold diggers after Geezers on Artificial Life Support (BIG GALS)

Bouncing Objects Seeking Old Men (BOSOM)

John Wayne Bobbitt

a.k.a. - "Frankenshlong"

Here is a man whose claim to fame was having his member dismembered. One minute he was yelling at his wife for sex, the next minute he thought he was in a deli providing the lunch meat. When Lorena tossed his sliced salami out of the car window, it was probably the most satisfaction she had ever received from it.

Lorena was acquitted when the evidence wouldn't stand up in court. (If you saw his porno movie you'd see that it didn't stand up too well there either.) His flick gave new meaning to the term "kinky sex" (in that he had sex with something that had a kink in it).

Casting Bobbitt as a porn star is like casting Sally Struthers as an aerobics instructor. While they may be capable of going through the motions, it makes us sick to watch.

Least favorite dessert: Banana split

Least favorite song: Mack the Knife

Likes: Microvascular surgery

Favorite toy: Erector set

Memberships: Individuals Making Love with Incapacitated Mangled Penises (I'M LIMP)

Society of the Castrated And Reattached (SCAR)

Theodore Kazynski

The Alleged Unabomber

You know a guy is dangerous when even postal workers are afraid of him.

Ted didn't always live in a shack with no running water. He used to have a nice house - but it got blown up when one of his packages was returned to sender.

The Unabomber threatened to kill again if The New York Times and Washington Post didn't publish his 10,000 word manifesto. They printed it in attempt to save lives, but ironically hundreds of their readers died of boredom.

Since his arrest, federal officials have been supplying Ted with his usual writing materials and are encouraging him to become pen pals with Fidel Castro, Saddam Hussein, and Muammar Qadafi.

Memberships: Kooks Allegedly Bombing Out Of Montana (KABOOM)

Joseph Hazelwood

Former Captain of the *Exxon Valdez*

Allegedly, this guy's breath was more flammable than the oil spilling out of his tanker. After the tanker ran aground, Hazelwood reportedly spewed out a stream of obscenities that made the *other* drunken sailors blush. Still, you've got to give him credit, after all, it seems he proved that all it takes to get water and oil to mix are a few bottles of alcohol.

Perhaps it was an instrument failure. It's possible the dipstick hanging off the port bow gave him a false reading that the Pacific Ocean was 10 million gallons low on oil.

While this was an ecological disaster, horrible things like this happen more frequently than we know. For example, the last time a million gallons of black, foul smelling sludge was released into the environment was when Marlon Brando drained his bath water.

Favorite movie: *The Poseidon Adventure*

Favorite musical: *Grease*

Favorite dessert: Baked Alaska

Favorite song: The Ballad of the Edmund Fitzgerald

Memberships: Organization Of Petroleum Spillers (OOPS)

Paula Jones

Former Arkansas state employee who claims that Bill Clinton was eager to "feel her pain" and asked if she was hurting underneath her lacy bra.

Her actual story is far worse. She claims that Bill Clinton cornered her in a hotel room, dropped his pants and told her to "kiss it." She politely declined, but decided years later to sue him.

Paula, it's impolite to "kiss and tell", but it's even worse to "not kiss it and tell." No one is interested in the fact that you *didn't* kiss it.

We're going to let you in on a little secret; *Any* woman, *any* where, at *any* time is invited to kiss any man's "it". It's a law of nature commonly known as the "Open Fly Rule."

Favorite song: Can't Touch This

Favorite TV show: *The Untouchables*

Favorite movie: *It*

Favorite quote: "When Bill said he had something big and stiff to show me, I thought he was going to introduce me to Al Gore."

Nicholas Leeson

a.k.a. - "Nickel-less" Leeson
a.k.a. - "Fleece 'em Leeson"

British banker. With all the caution and financial savvy of Ralph Kramden, he invested a fortune in the risky Asian marketplace. It all started off innocently enough; he lost one million here, 10 million there, pretty soon he was losing real money.

In buying up miles of prime swampland in Malaysia, falling prey to Japanese con artists who sold him the "Blooklyn Blidge" and cornering the market on magic beans, he lost $1.4 billion - effectively bankrupting the Barings Bank of Britain.

When bank bosses refused to accept his IOU, he was fired and brought up on charges. The only banks this guy will ever see again are on the sides of the river they sent him up.

Favorite magazine: Fortune telling 500

Favorite movie: *Other People's Money*

Favorite quote: "Buy low, sell high? **Now** they tell me!"

Memberships: Independent League Of Stock Exchange & Banking Industry Giants Buying Up Commonly Known Securities (I LOSE BIG BUCKS)

Entertainment
Losers

Michael Jackson

If Elvis knew his daughter was going to marry Michael Jackson, he would have requested that the sides of his coffin be greased (to make it easier for him to turn over in his grave).

Where else but in America could Michael Jackson have become a multimillionaire, loved by millions of adoring fans? In any other civilized country, a grown man who grabs his crotch in public, wears eyeliner and has slumber parties with little boys would be chased through the streets by an angry mob carrying torches and pitchforks.

Michael has had dozens of surgeries to fix his nose, his cheeks, his chin; but has refused surgery to fix the only thing that was ever *really* wrong with him - his brain.

Likes: Spanking his monkey
             Blowing Bubbles

Dislikes: Sniffing his glove

Turn ons: Underoos

Turn offs: Puberty

His biggest secret: When he grabs his crotch he *still* can't tell if he's a boy or a girl

Memberships: International Musicians Accused of Fondling and Reaching Ecstasy
                with Animals and Kids (I'M A FREAK)

Pee-Wee Herman

Many actors have put their blood, sweat and tears onto the big screen, but Pee-Wee got into trouble for putting another bodily fluid onto the screen from his seat in a XXX movie theater. After "Pee Wee's Big Top" made it to the theaters he never thought he would once again make it to the big screen, but he did, and from 20 rows back when his big top exploded.

While the other people in the audience cowered under raincoats (or at least covered the tops of their popcorn containers) three undercover detectives responded to a report that shots were being fired. They were shocked to find Pee-Wee red-faced and red-handed, not to mention left-handed. Thankfully, handcuffs were not necessary since Pee-Wee's hands were already sticking together.

While this may very well have been his best solo performance, Pee-Wee was arrested and received a slap on his already sore wrist instead of an Oscar.

Favorite song: Beat It

Favorite cookie: Oreos with Double Stuff

Favorite gas pump: Self service

Best career move: Pee-Wee's Playhouse

Worst career move: Pee-Wee's playing with himself in movie house

Chevy Chase

The King of Late Night Losers

Host of "The Chevy Chase Show"
a.k.a. - "Dead Man Talking"

His show was so painful to watch, that even insomniacs cried themselves to sleep. This show was so bad that the only reason it was closed captioned was so deaf people could hate it too. It's been said that when his show appeared on hospital TV's, patients awoke from comas just to change the channel.

In an attempt to alleviate the world's suffering, religious leaders put aside their differences to pray for "The Chevy Chase Show" to be canceled. Thankfully their prayers were answered, but not before Chevy left no doubt in anyone's mind that Gerald Ford was a better president than Chevy is a talk show host.

This show was *so* embarrassing that the town of Chevy Chase, Maryland is planning to legally change its name to Joe Piscopo and move to Delaware.

Dislikes: Anyone named Nielsen

Memberships: Inept Failures of Late night Obviously Poorly Programmed and Ending in Disaster (I FLOPPED)

Woody Allen

a.k.a. - "How Could He" Woody

His marital troubles with Mia began because she was always late for dinner and Woody always wanted to eat Soon. Hey Woody, the next time you're in the mood for Sum Yung Chik you better order out for it. Woody should try dating someone his own age, like maybe Yoko Ono.

Claim to fame: The only man in America who thinks Calvin Klein's models are too old.

Favorite TV shows: *All in the Family*
Family Affair
Father Knows Best
Make Room for Daddy

Favorite book: *Little Women*

Favorite song lyrics: "Oooo, me so horny."

Favorite play: *Miss Saigon*

Favorite drink: Shirley Temple

Favorite pick-up line: "You remind me of my daughter."

Memberships: Hot Old Repulsive Nerdy Yutzes Turned-on by Oriental Adopted Daughters (HORNY TOAD)

Godzilla

It has been announced that Godzilla will no longer appear in movies. His career is over. The ten-story tall, unemployed actor may now be reduced to standing on street corners with a sign that reads, "Will breathe fire for food."

Despite his apparent forced retirement, Godzilla still stands a better chance of making it back to the big screen than O.J. for the following reasons:

- While causing infinitely more destruction on miniaturized movie sets, Godzilla has never actually killed anyone.
- When the director says "cut", Godzilla knows it's just a figure of speech.

Likes: Stomping on Tokyo

Dislikes: Overgrown apes and flying reptiles
　　　　　　　Stepping on nail factories

Dislikes even more: When Mothra eats his sweaters

Favorite food: Flame broiled Japanese

Favorite dessert: Tums and a six pack of fire extinguishers

Favorite song: Walk the Dinosaur

Memberships: Big Awkward Dinosaurs Barbecuing, Roasting and Eating All of
　　　　　　　　Tokyo Heights (BAD BREATH)

Marlon Brando

It's sometimes difficult to tell whether he is a bitter, washed up actor, or a bloated, washed up sea mammal.

Brando starred in the original *Superman* movie as Superman's father, although most people think he played the exploding planet. In the movie *Don Juan DeMarco*, poor Faye Dunaway had to suffer through a love scene with Brando. The last time Hollywood put that much weight on top of one woman was when they dropped a house on The Wicked Witch of the East.

Brando reportedly owns his own island in the Pacific. Actually satellite photographs show that it's not an island at all - it's Brando floating on his back with a palm tree stuck in his belly button.

Favorite movie: *Willie Wonka and The Chocolate Factory*

Hobbies: Shifting the earth's center of gravity

Likes: Eating

Dislikes: Kosher food

Favorite desserts: Good Humor truck on a stick
Hershey, PA

Memberships: Flatulent Arrogant Thespians (FAT)
Society for Loudmouthed Overeating Bigots (SLOB)

Favorite song: *Eat It* (by Weird Al)

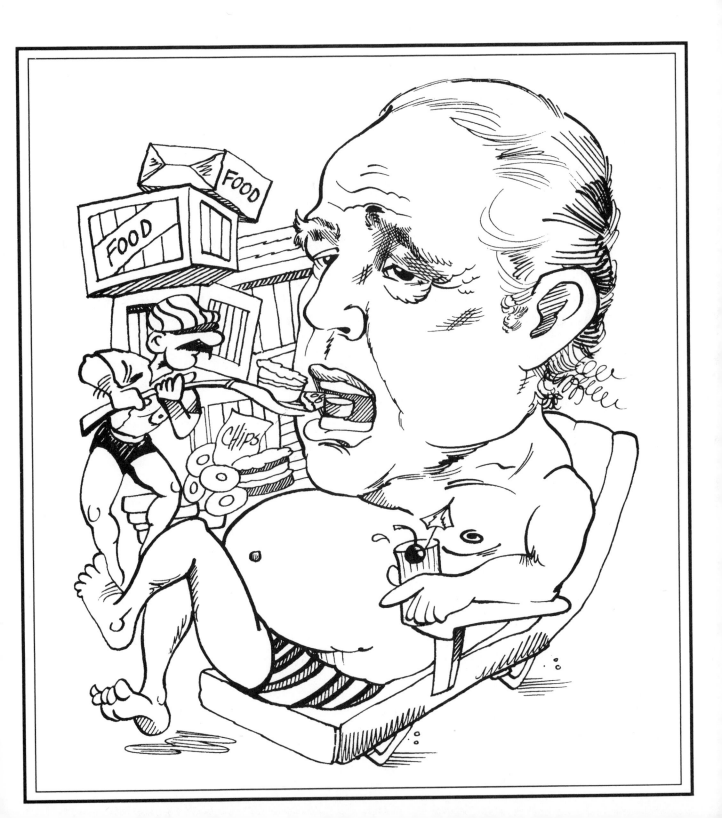

Hugh Grant

a.k.a. - "Hugh Dirty Dog, Hugh"

This British actor earned his 15 minutes of scorn by performing a lewd act in a pubic place in the front seat of a BMW with a hooker. Hugh, (who thinks "safe sex" means wearing a seat belt) was charged with indecency and improper merging.

Many believe that the whole ordeal was just a publicity stunt for his movie "Nine Months." Perhaps we can expect to see him in a movie starring himself, his prostitute, and eight of her friends in a movie titled, "Nine Mouths."

Favorite song: Paradise by the Dashboard Light

Second favorite song: Going Down (by the Monkees)

Favorite quote: "Could you give me two nipples for a dime?"

Favorite movies: Rob Lowe's collection of home videos

Favorite TV show: *T.J. Hooker*

Favorite deli meat: Tongue

Elizabeth Berkley

For over half a century the biggest disaster caught on tape was the explosion of the Hindenberg - that is until the movie *Showgirls* came out. This soft porn film about lap dancers couldn't have done any worse at the box office if it had starred Delta Burke (though technically it no longer would have been a movie about lap dancing, it would have been a movie about men's crushed pelvises).

It was a total bomb despite the fact that Siskel and Ebert left the theater with something other than their thumbs up.

Why go to a theater to shell out $7 to watch a movie about lap dancers when for $5 you can actually go to a strip joint, GET a lap dance and save money on popcorn?

Sorry Elizabeth, but this time your career was *not* saved by the bell. Who taught you how to move like a woman, Boy George? Look at the bright side, you will no longer have to strain your brain memorizing scripts - the only line you're going to need from now on is, "Ya want fries with that?"

Favorite Movie: *Striptease*

Biggest secret: Her acting coach was Mr. Ed

Charlie Sheen

a.k.a. - "John with Dough"

Paying over $53,000 for sex with 27 hookers earned Charlie a free trip "around the world" on Heidi Fleiss' Frequent Fornicator plan.

It may be hard to believe, but Charlie Sheen spends more money for sex than the federal government spends for toilet seats.

Just when we thought Charlie was straightening out, his marriage to a model broke up in only a few months, probably because she couldn't break him of the following habits:

- Asking, "How much extra is kissing?"
- Stuffing hundred dollar bills into her panties after sex.
- Making her dance around the bed in a cheerleaders uniform.

Likes: Anything dressed in a thong and rolling in a tub of lime Jell-O

Sports Hero: Wilt Chamberlain

Favorite quote: "Love means never having to say, 'do you take credit cards?'"

Sinead O'Connor

a.k.a. - "Baldy"

On *Saturday Night Live*, the one time popular singer shredded a picture of the Pope, and in doing so shredded her career. The only time anyone asks her for an autograph these days is when she's mistaken for Susan Powter's little sister.

Sinead did not intentionally go bald. She once had beautiful hair and in an attempt to make it more beautiful she used every hair care product on the market - even mixing them. Too bad she never closely read the directions which say "Harmful if swallowed."

Favorite actor: Yul Brenner

Favorite TV show: *Kojak*

Dislikes: Rapunzel

Dislikes even more: Being mistaken for "Mr. Clean"

Least Favorite Broadway Show: *Hair*

Least Favorite Song: The Star Spangled Banner

Memberships: Hair Club for Women

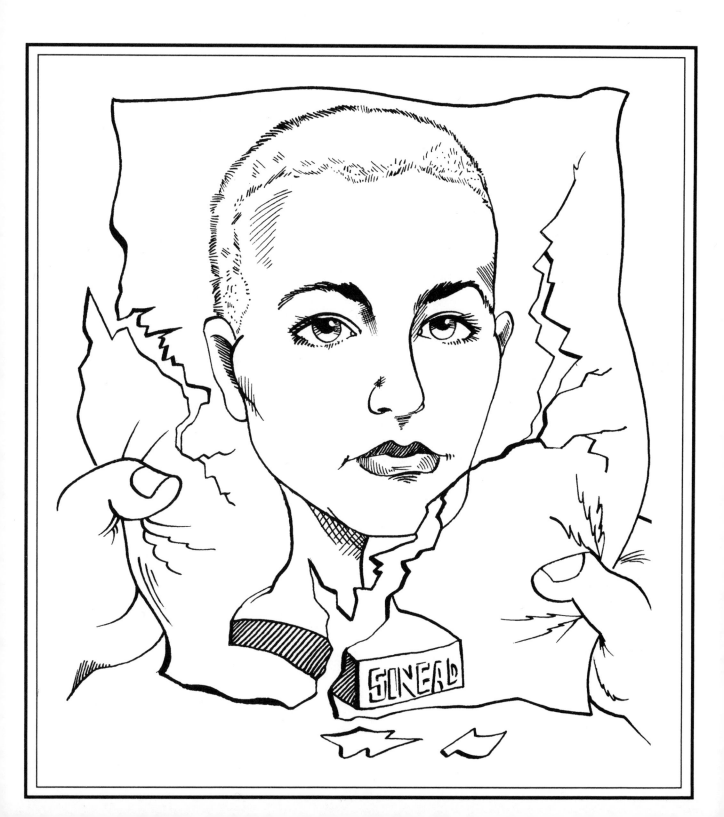

Babe

a.k.a. - "The Other White Meat"

The pig from down under has a better command of the English language than other comparable actors such as Flipper, Lassie and Pauly Shore.

Babe was nominated for several Oscars but was the winner of none. Unfortunately the Oscars do not yet have the category, "Actor who would make the best luncheon meat". Let's face it Babe; the day an Oscar judge tells you that you won an award for acting will be the day a rabbi tells you that you're Kosher for Passover.

Sorry Babe, but it seems the sty was the limit. Take heart, a talking pig hasn't won an Oscar since Marlon Brando.

Secret crush: Miss Piggy

Dislikes: Kermit
Open flames, Rotisseries, Apples
Pork rinds
Spam

Dislikes even more: Critics who call him a ham

Likes: Hamburgers

Courtney Love

Courtney made Time Magazine's list of the top 25 "Most Influential" people in America. She made our list of the top 25 people in America who are "Most under the Influence."

Her real talent is not in singing at concerts, it's in being able to stagger around on stage after taking enough drugs to kill every person in the first fifty rows. The last guy who pumped her stomach got so many drugs out he opened his own pharmacy.

Her singing has been likened to the sound of a dolphin passing a kidney stone. She is the only performer who dives off the stage into the crowd and the crowd throws her back.

Some religious leaders believe that the seventh sign of the apocalypse will be fulfilled, (and the world will end) when "The Courtney Love Singing School" opens up next door to the "Charles Nelson Reilly School of Performing Arts."

Least favorite song: "Love Stinks!"

Favorite movie: *Speed*

Favorite dessert: Uppers

Dislikes: Soap

Yoko Ono

a.k.a. - "The Roach who Married the Beatle"

Her "music" has been used for such diverse purposes as curing constipation, teaching dogs how to howl in pain and torturing political prisoners. However her records and CD's are most commonly used as table coasters and Frisbees.

When she's not busy offending people with her voice she's offending them by ripping pages out of bibles. She claims that she didn't know people would take offense to that because on her home planet of "Tone-deaf", they eat shredded bibles for breakfast.

Yoko lost her old band in a tragic accident (during one of her "singing" solos, each and every band member dropped to their knees and tore their own ears off). Since then, she has joined forces with her son Sean's band, Ima (which is a Japanese word meaning "Only the Deaf Shall Survive").

Favorite dessert: I scream

Hobbies: Slamming car doors on her fingers to perfect her singing technique

Political Losers

Dan Quayle

Formerly known as "Mr. Vice President"

The man who spent four years being "one heartbeat away from the presidency" has spent his whole life being one IQ point away from a baboon.

After taking on Murphy Brown for having a baby out of wedlock, he was all set to run for president as the "family values" candidate and promised to:

- Tackle those sluts Amanda and Allison of Melrose Place for sleeping with everyone west of the San Andreas fault.
- Start a letter writing campaign to get Al Bundy to drop his subscription to that porno magazine "Big 'uns."
- Have *E.R.*'s Dr. Doug Ross' medical license suspended for being a "whore - monger."

By the time it was explained to him that these people, these situations were not real, the shows were over and he was busy being offended by the next one.

Favorite toy: Mr. Potatoehead

Favorite quote: "Just say ... I don't no."

Memberships: Intellectually Challenged And Notoriously Thick Skulled Politicians Enraged by Leftist Liberals (I CAN'T SPELL)

Politicians Of Trivial Achievement Tarnishing Our English (POTATOE)

Pat Buchanan

Pat has repeatedly tried to capture the Republican presidential nomination with what he considers to be mainstream American thinking such as:

- The Ku Klux Klan is soft on immigrants.
- Homosexuals in the military can best serve their country as land mine sweepers.
- The only thing wrong with Mexico is that there are a bunch of Mexicans living there.
- The Theory of Evolution is complete utter hogwash, except for the fact that it explains how Blacks and Jews got here.

Thankfully, Pat has dropped his bid to run for President and instead has decided to run for God.

His Qualifications:
- He thinks he's God.
- He has condemned millions of people to Hell.
- He's good at making new commandments.

Likes: To hear himself talk

Dislikes: Too numerous too list

Memberships: Individuals Having Attitudes Towards Ethnic Undesirables
(I HATE U)

Favorite quote: "Give me your tired, huddled masses and I'll kick their tired, huddled asses!"

H. Ross Perot

American entrepreneur / politician / loony tune

His Reform party used to be called the "United We Stand" party (shortened from its full name - "United We Stand to Benefit a Great Deal from Electroshock Therapy"). No matter what he calls it, his party seems to uphold the great American values of fear, distrust and paranoia.

With all the charm, intelligence and warmth of a yapping Chihuahua he alternates between telling us about the "crazy aunt" he has locked in the basement and diving beneath tables screaming "The Libyans are NAFTA me!!"

We know you want to be President, but don't get your hopes up Ross. When the American people say they want an outsider for President, they mean someone who is out of the Beltway, not out of his mind.

Dislikes: Being mistaken for Frank Purdue

Dislikes even more: Rumors that his daughter is dating Newt's sister

Favorite movie: *Dumbo*

Likes: Q-tips

Favorite quote: "It takes a tough man to make a tender country."

Marion Barry

Formerly known as, "The Disgraced Crack Addict."
Now known as "The Honorable, Distinguished
Crack Addict Mayor of Washington, D.C."

The good things about having Marion Barry for mayor:

- Money is saved by having the mayor's office share space with the city's rehab center.
- He lets the D.C. Police Force use his house to train their drug sniffing dogs.

Likes: Smoking crack

Dislikes: Getting caught

Favorite song: I Want a New Drug

Least favorite movie: The FBI surveillance tapes

Favorite quote: "The bitch set me up."

Second favorite quote: "Guard, I'll give you the key to the city if you give me the key to my jail cell."

Party Affiliation: Democrack

Memberships: Society of Crack Using Mayors (SCUM)

Bob Packwood

a.k.a. - "Bob Sixpackwood"

The former U.S. Senator has been accused of grabbing and groping every female who *ever* came within his grasp (with the exception of Janet Reno). Packwood often escaped detection by claiming he had simply been mistaken for Ted Kennedy.

After years of jumping up on women, drooling and slobbering, female staffers didn't know if they were working for a Senator or a St. Bernard. His downfall was in trying to hold on to the memories by keeping a diary and a panty collection.

After his fingerprints were found on the hem of every dress and on the buttons of every blouse in Washington, Bob was forced to resign his seat and give up his bid to establish a new Senate Sub-committee on Bras and Breasts.

Favorite candy: Mounds

Favorite TV show: *Bosom Buddies*

Favorite restaurant: Hooters

Memberships: Big Over-sexed Tushy Touching Officials Making Stupid Unwanted Passes (BOTTOMS UP)

Favorite Quote: "Give me liberty or give me breasts."

Favorite song: I Want Your Sex

Ted Kennedy

Also sometimes answers to - "Hey Pal, I said last call!"

As a senior, seldom sober Senator, the only thing Ted abuses more than his power is his liver. Why do the good people of Massachusetts keep re-electing him? Because they know that if he wasn't in the Senate, he would be in their driveways and alleys rummaging through their garbage cans looking for booze.

According to conservatives, the only thing worse than Ted's voting record is his driving record. This may explain why the only thing Ted fears more than the Republicans is a breathalyzer. Still the hard drinking will pay off in the long run. Ted has pickled himself so well there is no doubt his body will be preserved longer than King Tut's.

It's too bad Ted never pursued a movie career. He would have made a great leading man - if they ever made a movie titled, "Driving Miss Daisy off The Bridges of Madison County."

Favorite movie: *Cocktail*

Favorite TV show: *The Underwater Adventures of Jacques Costeau*

Likes: Bars, bartenders, bar stools, barmaids, barfing

Dislikes: When he's six steps into a 12 step program and starts staggering again

Favorite quote: "Officer, I'm not drunk, I'm Ted Kennedy."

Second favorite quote: "I'll drive off that bridge when I get to it."

Memberships: Democrats United against Intolerance (DUI)
Liberals with Unhealthy Sick Habits (LUSH)

Jesse Helms

a.k.a. - "Yes'm Massa"

U.S. Senator from North Carolina. Helms thinks the only thing wrong with the tobacco industry is that there are no longer any slaves to work the fields. Some people believe Helms' deeply rooted support for cigarettes stems from the fact that smoking is pretty much the only pleasurable thing he can still do in bed.

During his time in the senate, Helms has lobbied behind the scenes to:

- Replace the Bald Eagle with Joe Camel.
- Change the Statue of Liberty's torch to a cigarette lighter.
- Change the name of "The United States of America" to "Marlboro Country."

Favorite song: Puff (The Magic Dragon)

Dislikes: Fresh air

The Emancipation Proclamation

The fact that the "Old South" stands a better chance of rising again than he does

Memberships: Congressional Republicans And Conservatives Keeping to the Extreme Right (CRACKER)

Newt Gingrich

a.k.a. - "The Speaker of the House"

No other congressman can spout off like Newt, because no other congressman has a blow hole like Newt. Newt takes the knee out of knee-jerk Republicanism. With the same zeal and conviction Sally Struthers uses to beg for food, Newt preaches for his various causes such as:

- Sending welfare mothers to Siberia.
- Auctioning orphans to the highest bidder (as slaves or perhaps, as appetizers).
- Reducing the national debt by selling the internal organs of illegal aliens.
- Outfitting Air Force One with an extra large back seat and a pork rind vending machine.

Newt was offered a $4.5 million book advance (which is *much* more than Hemingway, Dickens or Shakespeare were ever offered). Obviously Newt is some literary genius (despite the fact that *his* exposure to literature has been limited to reading the backs of cereal boxes and Twinkie wrappers).

Dislikes: Connie Chung

Dislikes even more: The fact that his sister has slept with more women than he has.

Favorite food: Chicken - Right Wing Only

His biggest secret: Newt is short for Neutered.

Memberships: Politics In Georgia Society (PIGS)
Big Obnoxious Arrogant Republicans (BOAR)

Joycelyn Elders

U.S. physician and public official. For a woman who prides herself on the merits of masturbation, she sure knows how to rub people the wrong way.

Dr. Elders proposed that children should be taught how to masturbate in school (presumably this would be taught in association with a class on thorough hand washing).

Lesser known was her private campaign to appoint Pee-Wee Herman as the nation's first "masturbation czar" - because he seemed to have such a firm grasp on the issue.

Fortunately, Clinton had the good sense to dump Elders before he had to print a warning label to stick across her butt reading:

"**The Surgeon General is hazardous to your health**."

Favorite quote: "One in the hand beats any in the bush."

Favorite food: Creamed corn

Dislikes: The fact that while she may be the doctor in the house, everyone goes to her son when they need drugs.

Memberships: Individuals Meaning to Advance Sensuous Touching Until Reactive Body Areas Totally Explode (I MASTURBATE)

Michael Dukakis

In choosing Dukakis as a presidential candidate in 1988, Democrats made a statement that they wanted to revive the politics of the past. No, not the old 60's type liberalism, but the old Aztec custom of offering a blood sacrifice to the gods.

The Democrats might as well have tied Dukakis to a sacrificial altar on a mountain top and ripped out his beating heart. At least then he might've gotten the sympathy vote. Bush gave Dukakis the kind of political mauling seldom seen between politicians in captivity. By election day Bush had everyone convinced that Dukakis' vice presidential running mate was Willie Horton.

Unlike his famous relative, Olympia, Michael's acting career ended abruptly when he stormed off the set of the Wizard of Oz after running for Mayor of Munchkinland and losing the election by a landslide.

Favorite quote: "I AM Standing!"

Favorite dessert: Strawberry Shortcake

Dislikes: Plucking his eyebrows

Dislikes even more: Being mistaken for a werewolf

Hobbies: Throwing his dirty socks into Boston Harbor

Memberships: Individuals Cast Away Never to Take Washington in November
(I CAN'T WIN)

David Duke

Former Ku Klux Klan leader / Respected Louisiana politician

a.k.a. - "The Boy in the Hood"

Duke has promised that if he is elected to public office he will pay close attention to detail, including dotting the i's and burning the crosses. On national holidays, this super patriot not only hangs the flag from his porch, but also a few ethnic undesirables from his trees.

It has been rumored that Duke had extensive plastic surgery in response to the fact that Michael Jackson was becoming whiter than he was.

Favorite quote: "Get your cotton pickin' hands off me."

Second favorite quote: "If you can't stand the heat, get off your lawn."

Least favorite aunt: Jemima

Least favorite uncle: Ben

Favorite uncle: Tom

Favorite bumper sticker: I Brake for Whites.

Favorite TV show: *Crossfire*

Memberships: Lowlife Yahoos Needing Costumes & Hoods Made Of Bed sheets (LYNCHMOB)

Mel Reynolds

Former Congressman from Illinois

Old state motto: Land of Lincoln
New state motto: Land in the Back Seat of My Lincoln

Reynolds got into trouble for taking Ma Bell's advice too seriously when he reached out and touched an under age campaign worker. It seems even phone sex isn't safe if you're a Congressman. This guy is like Joey Buttafuoco with a calling card.

Convicted on charges of sexual misconduct, witness tampering, and child pornography, the hardest thing for him to do was give up his seat in Congress, mostly because he was sticking to it.

What The Phone Company Calls it....	**What Mel Reynolds Calls it....**
Rotary dialing	Foreplay
Speed dialing	A Quickie
A toll free call	A Freebie
Three way calling	Menage-a-trois
Conference calling	An Orgy
Being disconnected	Coitus Interruptus
*69	69
A busy signal	She's cheatin' on me !

Dan Rostenkowski

Formerly known in Congress as "Mr. Chairman."
Now known in jail as "Mr. Butterbuns."

Getting Rostenkowski to plead guilty to charges of mail fraud is like getting the Hillside Strangler to plead guilty to double parking. This guy stole over $600,000 from American taxpayers and they nail him for swiping a few too many Marilyn Monroe stamps for his "personal use" (perhaps explaining why all the glue was licked off of them).

For the offense of mail fraud he was sentenced to 17 months in jail. He should just be grateful he was sentenced by the Justice Department rather than by the Postal Service (who had their crack team of disgruntled sharpshooters on standby).

Favorite quote (while in Congress): "Everyone does it."

Favorite quote (while in jail): "Oww!! You're hurting my prostate!"

Favorite song: The Fool on the Hill

Memberships: Lying Immoral Congressman Knowing That He Is a Scapegoat (LICK THIS)

Legal Losers

The O.J. Criminal Trial Jurors

a.k.a. - "Twelve Blind Mice"

Considering the verdict they reached, there is no doubt that O.J. was indeed tried by a jury of his peers - morons. So what if the cops were racists? So what if the glove may have been planted? That doesn't change the fact that there was so much of O.J.'s blood at the crime scene it's a miracle *he* didn't bleed to death there himself.

In the days since they bought the defense arguments, several jurors have accepted offers to buy:

- The Brooklyn Bridge
- Beach front property in South Dakota
- Bonds from Michael Milken

After nine months of trial, the jury spent only four hours locked in deliberation. Reportedly the jurors, (who were deliberating through the dinner hour) spent at least three hours arguing over which toppings they were going to have on their pizza and were deadlocked on the issue of whether the crust should be thick or thin.

Like: Johnny Cochran's rhymes

Dislike: Evidence, facts, truth

Dislike even more: Justice

Memberships: Jurors Eager to Release Killers (JERKs)

Erik & Lyle Menendez

a.k.a. - "The Self-Made Orphans"

These poor little rich boys made their parents' low fat, low cholesterol diet worthless with a few blasts from a shotgun, horrifying everyone in the civilized world. Even Charles Manson doesn't kill members of his own family. F. Lee Bailey and Johnnie Cochran were also disgusted with the boys' behavior, (not the fact that they blew their parents away, but the fact that they blew so much money before their trial that they couldn't afford to hire them).

The boys later claimed they were sexually abused by their parents. If they think sexual abuse by their parents was bad, it was just a warm up for what these pretty boys can expect in prison every night for the rest of their lives. Even if they were sexually abused by their parents, they were better off than they are now - at least their parents loved them.

Hobbies: Sitting-duck hunting

Motto: Shoot first, make accusations later.

Memberships: Co-Presidents of the Lizzie Borden fan club
Brothers Lacking Any Scruples Together Executing Mom & dad (BLAST 'EM)

Leona Helmsley

a.k.a. - "The Queen of Mean"

Calling Leona "cheap" is like calling Jabba The Hutt "chubby." Both are gross understatements (with the emphasis on gross). She's so tight fisted, that her employees frequently need paramedics to use the "Jaws of Life" to pry their paychecks out of her hands.

Despite her reputation, she actually paid over $50 million in taxes to the government - and what did they do in appreciation? Give her a ticker tape parade? Name a space shuttle after her? NO, they throw her in jail for five years! NOW THAT'S what we call a LOSER!

After her fancy hotel pampered life, the hardest thing for Leona to get used to in jail was the fact that they didn't put mints on her pillows.

As a matter of fact, the only things that prison and her hotel have in common are that they both have a nice view of the river.

Dislikes: Paying taxes, making own bed

Favorite quote: "Only little people pay taxes."

Hobbies: Wrestling pennies away from blind panhandlers.
Swiping the cheese from mouse traps.

Mark Fuhrman

a.k.a. - "The Fuhrer-man"

Was this man a reliable investigator and witness?
You be the judge!

Consider the facts:

- He swears under oath that he has never used the "n" word, (except maybe for the few hundred times he said it on tape and every time he swung his night stick at an African-American).

- He sometimes confuses his edition of the LAPD regulations handbook with Mein Kampf.

- He conducted the most bungled criminal investigation in L.A. since the Keystone Cops.

- The last time a man of his beliefs took the stand was at Nuremberg.

Favorite dessert: Ice cream - Vanilla only

Likes: To hate

Dislikes: Having only eight bullets in his gun when stopping a van that has nine black "suspects".

Favorite movie: The Rodney King video

Least favorite song: Ebony & Ivory

Hobbies: Planting flowers, vegetables, bloody gloves

F. Lee Bailey

a.k.a. - "F. Lee Not out on Bailey"

It's amazing that a guy who calls himself a criminal lawyer has never defended a criminal in his whole life. All his clients seem to be innocent! Which appears to be more than we can say for him. After all, Bailey has probably served more time than most of his clients.

He spends most of his time with low life, degenerate, scum of the earth piles of protoplasm who would cut our throats without a morsel of remorse - and those are just the other O.J. legal defense "dream team" members.

Dislikes: Dirty drug money

Likes: Clean, laundered drug money

Dislikes: Poor, low-down, lying, stealing, murdering, sleazeballs

Likes: Rich, low-down, lying, stealing, murdering, sleazeballs

Favorite quote: "O.J.'s innocent and the money is mine".

Memberships: Sub-Human Yutzes Securing Throatslashers' Early Release (SHYSTER)

Creeps Representing Obnoxious Obvious Killers (CROOK)

Stacy Koon &
Laurence Powell

a.k.a. - "The High Kicking, Rodney Rockettes"

These cops were eventually sentenced to 30 months in prison for violating Rodney King's civil rights, (which evidently include his right to drink & drive, speed through a residential neighborhood at 100 m.p.h., violate parole and resist arrest).

We hope you guys learned a valuable lesson from all this. The next time you go on a beating spree, be sure to start with the guy who has the video camera.

If you find in the future that you *must* beat a belligerent motorist senseless, make it that cop-slapper, Zsa-Zsa Gabor. She offers the following advantages to beating Rodney King:

- No one will care.
- Half of the city won't be burned down when you get acquitted.
- You won't have to use "excessive force" to break her bones.
- You can send her a bill after the beating. After all, this is a woman who is probably used to paying for having her face re-arranged.

Memberships: Street Tough Officers Menacing Punks (STOMP)

Bernard Goetz

a.k.a. - "The Subway Vigilante"
a.k.a. - "The Geek with the Gun"

When approached on a New York City subway by four hoodlums and asked for $5, Goetz, (being a generous man) responded by giving them $10, (worth of lead). In a hail of bullets fired at point blank range, he seriously injured one of the punks. After the shootings, some people accused him of having murderous racist tendencies and paranoid delusions; others accused him of having REALLY bad aim and not enough ammunition.

Twelve years later, after losing a civil suit, Goetz had the honor to become the first mugging victim in the world to have been robbed in court by a jury ordering him to pay one of his attackers $43 million. How's that? It seems Goetz is much better at defending himself on the subway than in the courtroom. With lines like, "You don't look so bad, here's another," Goetz did more damage shooting off his mouth than shooting off his gun.

Favorite movies: *Death Wish, Death Wish II, III, IV & V*
Falling Down

Least favorite song: I Fought the Law and the Law Won

Favorite quote: "Go ahead...make my day."

Favorite food: Swiss cheese

Dislikes: Powder burns

Memberships: Extremely Armed Train riders Looking to Eliminate Aggressive Delinquents (EAT LEAD)

Sports
Losers

Tonya Harding

a.k.a. - "The Queen of Clubs"

Whether she's denying involvement in having someone's knee cap broken, crying to Olympic officials about her laces, or being booed off stage during a short singing career, there is something for everyone to hate about Tonya.

After the Kerrigan incident, in a classic example of the skate being on the other foot, Tonya herself was the victim of an attack at an Oregon park. Unfortunately, her attacker was never found, (probably because it was too hard to narrow the search down to one suspect out of the 4 billion people in the world who hate her).

On the ice, she is the only figure skater that even hockey players are afraid of. At the '94 Olympics, Tonya blew her chance at winning a medal in Skating, but her performance *did* earn her gold, silver and bronze medals in the categories of crying, whining and complaining - all because she can't tie her own shoelaces.

Favorite drink: Club soda

Nancy Kerrigan

a.k.a. - "The Ice Queen"

After Tonya's ex-husband and his goons smashed her knee she had our sympathy. At the Olympics she had our support. When she came back with a silver medal, she had us eating out of her hands.

Then she did the unthinkable - she dissed Disney. All she had to do was shut up and wave, and she could have been America's sweetheart, but no. While we were trying to pay homage to our new "Cinderella" she acted more like the wicked stepmother saying the Main Street parade was "corny."

She might as well have stomped on an apple pie, spit on a Chevrolet, burned a flag and kicked a bald eagle. She has proved that it doesn't take a brain surgeon to skate well, it doesn't even take a brain.

Favorite quote: "M-I-C, K-E-Y me, oh, why me? This is corny".

Favorite dessert: Sugar cube

Likes: Night clubs

Dislikes: Metal clubs

Least favorite place: Wounded Knee

Mike Tyson

a.k.a. - "Iron Mike"
a.k.a. - "Jail House Rocky"

If ever there was a loser at love, Mike is it. His stormy, short lived marriage to Robin Givens taught Mike that the way to a woman's heart is to punch your way through her rib cage.

Later, he was convicted of raping a beauty pageant contestant when his legal defense team failed to convince a jury that if she *really* wanted him to get off of her, she would have rung a bell or thrown a towel on to the bed.

In jail, Mike converted to Islam but doesn't go by his Islamic name because it's too hard for him to spell.

Likes: A woman's tender touch

Dislikes: Getting lipstick on his knuckles

Favorite quote: "The prettier they are, the harder they fall."

Favorite sports figure: O.J.

Memberships: World champion Heavyweights who Allegedly Clobber women with their Knuckles (WHACK)

Peter McNeeley

Formerly known as, "The Great White Hope."
Now known as, "The Beaten to a Pulp."

This guy shouldn't be boxing, he should be doing something he has REAL talent for, like donating blood.

In a championship bout against Mike Tyson, McNeeley became the undisputed "Heavyweight Loser of the World" in only 89 seconds. The only BIGGER Losers were pay-per-view subscribers.

Likes: Throwing in towels

Dislikes: The taste of canvas, the number 10, spitting out teeth

Favorite dessert: Marshmallow treats

Least favorite movie: *Rocky*

Least favorite song: We Are the Champions

Favorite TV show: *Saved by the Bell*

Favorite song: Hit me with your Best Shot

Favorite sandwich: Knuckle

Favorite quote: "OK, so Mike knocked me down, at least he didn't rape me."

Marge Schott

Suspended owner of the Cincinnati Reds. She describes Adolph Hitler as not only a great man, but a helluva third baseman in his day. Many psychologists believe that her pre-occupation with Nazi ideals may stem from her resemblance to a World War II battle tank.

On the baseball diamond, Schott doesn't want to just win, she wants to conquer. If she had things her way, following a victory, she would make the other team's coach sign a formal document of surrender - then round up the defeated players and take them to a P.O.W. camp.

Favorite possession: A Nazi armband (worn only on "special occasions" such as weddings, funerals, cross burnings).

Favorite quote: "Today Cincinnati, tomorrow the world!"

Favorite song: Springtime for Hitler

Pet Peeve: She'd like to find the commie who named her team the "Reds."

Memberships: Grandmothers Everywhere Seeking The Annihilation of People Other than white (GESTAPO)

Royal Losers

Prince Charles

a.k.a. - "The Duke of Dumbo"

Charles was formerly known as "The Man Who Would Be King", but is now known as "His Royal Hiney" (because the only throne he'll ever sit on will be made of porcelain). He is best known for ditching his wife (the young, hot, blue-blooded babe, Lady Di) for his mistress (the old, cold, blue-skinned bloodhound, Camilla Parker Bowles).

Is it possible that his ears are so very large to compensate for his incredibly poor eyesight?! As if trading in a fox for a hound isn't bad enough, it cost him $26.4 million in the divorce settlement to do it.

Charles is a shining example to Losers everywhere that it is possible to overcome the considerable obstacles of immense wealth and royal lineage to become a World Class Loser.

Favorite quote: "I don't care if you CAN see France on the other side, that's not the chunnel, that's my ear canal!"

Second Favorite quote: "That's not the Queen Mum, that's my mistress!"

Favorite song lyrics: "If you want to be happy for the rest of your life (never make a pretty woman your wife)."

Dislikes: Dog whistles

Memberships: Individuals Having Extraordinary Auditory Reception Acquired by Large Lobes (I HEAR ALL)

Sarah Ferguson

a.k.a. - Fergie
a.k.a. - The Duchess of Pork
a.k.a. - The Duchess of Whales
Formerly known as "Her Royal Highness."
Now known as "Her Thunder Thighness."

Prince Andrew was so rich, charming and handsome, he could easily have gotten his milk for free - so why did he marry the cow?

With her well known habit of spending more money than she makes, Fergie is better suited to be a member of the U.S. Congress than the British royal family.

Fergie's financially troubled "Budgie the Helicopter" line of children's books and merchandising has shown kids that even a cute, cartoon helicopter can crash and burn.

Her lesser known, first line of children's books, (based on a *fictional* character) called "Fudgie - the Redheaded, Adulterous, Royal Slut and a Half" also failed to captivate the imagination of British children.

Likes: All-u-can-eat breakfast buffets

Dislikes: The Thighmaster
          When kids stop, point at her and scream "Mad Cow!"

Favorite movie: *The Battle of the Bulge*

Queen Elizabeth

a.k.a. - "The Mother of all Royal Losers"

Where invading armies, plagues and famines have failed; one woman's batch of bad eggs has finally succeeded in putting an end to the British monarchy.

One would think that the richest woman in the world could have afforded to adopt a few children. Her offspring (Charles & Andrew - a.k.a. Dumb & Dumber) are much better suited to carry on in the tradition of Barnum & Bailey's traveling freak show than the proud tradition of the British monarchy.

Certainly this travesty of biology was not her fault. Who could've known that wearing $30 million worth of gems during pregnancy could damage the royal family jewels? Or did she just live too close to the royal power lines?

Dislikes: Washing behind Charles' ears

Dislikes even more: Daughter-in-laws

Hobbies: Arm Wrestling, Bowling, Checking the Queen Mum's pulse

World Leader Losers

Saddam Hussein

a.k.a. - "The Butcher of Baghdad"

He promised then President Bush the "Mother of all Wars", but after a beating called "Desert Storm", Hussein ended up running home to his mother.

For 100 hours, high tech cruise missiles, planes, tanks and aircraft carriers rained down destruction on Hussein's armies of unshaven, half-starved, bed wetters and armor plated camels. Ignoring outcries from world leaders to stop the carnage, President Bush finally ceased firing on the Iraqis in response to impassioned pleas from environmentalists, (who pointed out that for every Iraqi soldier killed or captured, ten thousand Iraqi fleas were made homeless).

It is rumored that during the height of the bombing, Saddam was stuck in a bunker that had no toilet paper - so for a few days the "Butcher of Baghdad" had more than just blood on his hands.

Turn ons: The smell of camels

Turn offs: The smell of Iraqi women

Favorite movie: *Ishtar*

Favorite music: Screams from political prisoners in torture chambers
Any Yoko Ono Album

Favorite quote: "I dare you to cross this line...OK, I dare you to cross *this* line."

Memberships: Stupid Leaders In the Middle East (SLIME)

Manuel Noriega

Formerly known throughout the world as "The Strongman of Panama" he is now known throughout the federal penitentiary as "The cute guy in cell 32A". The biggest worry of the former dictator who lost his grip on power is that he might lose his grip on the soap while in the shower.

To put an end to Panama's drug dealing, money laundering and silly belief that it was sovereign and independent, the United States invaded in 1989. Actually the Pentagon only dispatched a den mother and a troop of cub scouts armed with Supersoakers and a "G.I. Joe with the Kung Fu Grip." Nevertheless, the ensuing "war" was quicker and used less force than it took to subdue Rodney King.

As the former leader of a run down, drug infested, lawless society, the only two things Noriega is qualified to do in the U.S. are:

1) Rot in jail, or
2) be the mayor of Washington, D.C.

Likes: Oxy 10

Dislikes: Being called "Pineapple face."

Favorite quote: "I am not an animal, I'm a human being!"

Muammar Qadafi

a.k.a. - "The Lunatic of Libya"

Muammar is an old Arabic word which roughly translated means:

"He who is one hump short of a camel."

After Libya proudly sponsored World Terrorism the way normal countries sponsor the Olympics, President Reagan ordered a bombing, (dubbed Operation "Desert Scum") which remodeled Qadafi's house.

Reconnaissance and Satellite surveillance of Libya show a country that looks like a 50,000 square mile box of kitty litter except that no one bothered to cover Qadafi with sand.

What he's building....

Supergun
Nuclear power plant
Chemical weapons plant
His bathroom

What he's calling it...

Super salad-shooter
Tanning salon
Perfume factory
Biological weapons plant

Memberships: Brotherhood of Oil-rich Maniacal Bullies of the Middle East (BOMB ME)

Fidel Castro

In Spanish, Fidel means: "He whose people feed the sharks."

It must get lonely as the only communist in the Western Hemisphere, especially since someone cut the string on the tin can connected to Moscow.

As the undisputed leader of the "Third World", the only reason Fidel has such a bushy beard is because Cuba ran out of razor blades thirty years ago.

Being deprived of the sex, violence and displays of material wealth found on American TV, the Cubans produce their own inferior, communist versions of our shows such as:

Our show	Their show
Friends	Comrades
Baywatch	Bay of Pigs
Eight is Enough	You Ate Enough

Favorite quote: "Yes, I am happy to see you, but that *is* a gun in my pocket."

Memberships: Impoverishing Millions And Confiscating Others' Money Made by Independent Enterprises (I'M A COMMIE)

Idi Amin

Idi is an old African word meaning, "I'm hungry."

Formerly known as the President of Uganda, Idi is best known for maintaining a diet that would make Hannibal Lechter look like a vegetarian. Unlike China, (which limits population growth by allowing one child per couple) Idi is rumored to have kept the population of his country under control by eating excess people.

The high point of his political career was allowing one planeload of Israeli commandos to take over his country in 30 minutes. Who trained his army, the French?

Favorite quote: "I love my people - medium rare."

Second favorite quote: "Tastes like chicken."

Favorite movie: *Eating Raoul*

Least favorite movie: *Raid on Entebbe*

Favorite *Twilight Zone* episode: "To Serve Man"

Pet Peeve: "Shake & Bake" bags are too small

AMERICA'S FAVORITE
SUPERZERO™
CAPTAIN LOSER™
IS LOOKING FOR LOSERS!

With the help of Major Loser™and Lt. Loser™, Captain Loser™ has been ordered by the Joint Chiefs of Losers to find the World's Biggest Loser!

We're sure you know at least one person who might be it!

Maybe it's your boss, your neighbor, your ex, someone you dated, a relative - whoever the Loser is, you have a duty to report them at once to Captain Loser. Tell him, in writing, what they did to deserve the title, "World's Biggest Loser."

You will be doing mankind and your country a great service. If we agree that your loser is a serious contender for the title, (after changing names and locations) we will profile *your* Loser in the next *Who's Who of Losers.*™ We will also send *you* an International Losers Club T-shirt! (All submitted material becomes the property of the International Losers Club).

E mail:

captloser@losersclub.com

Or write to:

Captain Loser™
c/o The International Losers Club
350 Fifth Avenue - Suite 3304
New York, NY 10118-0069

CAPTAIN LOSER™

Losers of the World Unite!
Join the Club!

For membership information write to:

The International Losers Club
EMPIRE STATE BUILDING
350 Fifth Avenue - Suite 3304
New York, NY 10118-0069

or E-mail:

loser@losersclub.com

Losers on the Net

www.losersclub.com

Check it out! It's hot! It's cool! It's the place Losers rule! Join us at the 24 hour on-line Loser-fest in cyberspace! It's the place to turn for all your important Loser information from the World's foremost authority - **The International Losers Club**.

Humor Writers,
We Want You !

Have other publishers treated <u>you</u> like a Loser? We won't! We are looking for talented comedy writers. We don't care if you have an agent, we don't care if you're in an institution. If your friends tell you you're funny and:

- They're not talking about the way you look.
- You can be funny ON PAPER!

Then we want to hear from you!

Gordon Entertainment Multimedia, Inc. is seeking humor / comedy writers for future projects including books, radio and recording, television, and movie screenplays. If you're looking for highly satisfying, part time, freelance work, send us a sample. We **will** read your work. You may qualify to join our team of writers.

Gordon Entertainment Multimedia, Inc.
EMPIRE STATE BUILDING
350 Fifth Avenue - Suite 3304
New York, NY 10118-0069

E-mail: Gordonentm@aol.com

Index of Losers